DELANEY
STREET
PRESS

Teachers Change the World . . . One Student at a Time

Nine Timeless Lessons That Extend Beyond the Classroom

Dr. Criswell Freeman

DELANEY STREET PRESS
Nashville, TN: 1-800-256-8584

ISBN: 1-58334-067-X

The ideas expressed in this book are not, in all cases, exact quotations, as some have been edited for clarity and brevity. In all cases, the author has attempted to maintain the speaker's original intent. In some cases, material for this book was obtained from secondary sources, primarily print media. While every effort was made to ensure the accuracy of these sources, the accuracy cannot be guaranteed. For additions, deletions, corrections or clarifications in future editions of this text, please write DELANEY STREET PRESS.

Printed in the United States of America
Cover Design by Bart Dawson
Typesetting & Page Layout by Swan Lake Communications,
Jackson, Mississippi

1 2 3 4 5 6 7 8 9 10 • 00 01 02 03 04 05 06

ACKNOWLEDGMENTS

The author gratefully acknowledges the support of Angela Beasley Freeman, Dick and Mary Freeman, Mary Susan Freeman, Jim Gallery, and the team of helpful professionals at Walnut Grove Press and Delaney Street Press.

For Those Who Care Enough
to Teach

Table of Contents

If we work in marble,
it will perish; if we work
upon brass, time will efface it;
if we rear temples, they
will crumble into dust;
but if we work upon immortal
minds and instill in them
just principles, we are then
engraving upon tablets
which no time will efface,
but will brighten and
brighten to all eternity.

DANIEL WEBSTER

Introduction

Henry Brooks Adams correctly observed, "A teacher affects eternity; he can never tell where his influence stops."

All of us remember special teachers, caring men and women who taught lessons that have lasted a lifetime. In this book we will examine nine such lessons. Using the quotations of notable men and women, we will examine nine powerful principles that extend far beyond the classroom.

Teachers change the world by changing their students. The late Bart Giamatti observed, "Teachers believe they have a gift for giving; it drives them with the same irrepressible drive that drives others to create a work of art, or a marker, or a building."

On the pages that follow, we celebrate the enduring artwork of those master teachers whose reach extends beyond time and place. Great teachers mold eternity, and this little book shows how they do it.

LESSON #1

The Power
of Education

Teachers understand the value of education. Students often do not. Thus, the first lesson that a good teacher must often teach is the importance of education.

Education is the tool by which we come to know and appreciate the world in which we live. It is the shining light that snuffs out the darkness of ignorance and poverty. Education is freedom just as surely as ignorance is a form of bondage.

The following quotations reinforce a message that teachers know all too well: Education is not a luxury, it is a necessity and a powerful tool for good in this world.

Teaching is not the
filling of the pail
but the lighting
of the fire.

WILLIAM BUTLER YEATS

The educated
differ from the
uneducated as much
as the living from
the dead.

Aristotle

Education is the process by
which the individual relates
himself to the universe, gives
himself citizenship in the
changing world, and shares
the human race's mind.

Dr. John H. Finley

Education is the mother
of leadership.

Wendell Willkie

The purpose of learning is
growth, and our minds, unlike
our bodies, can continue to
grow as we continue to live.

Mortimer Adler

The empires of
the future are
the empires
of the mind.

WINSTON CHURCHILL

Education's purpose is
to replace an empty mind
with an open one.

Malcolm Forbes

We shouldn't teach great
books; we should teach
a love of reading.

B. F. Skinner

He knows enough
who knows how to learn.

Henry Adams

Education is the best provision for old age.

Aristotle

Learning is not attained by chance. It must be sought for with ardor and attended to with diligence.

Abigail Adams

It is what we think we know already that prevents us from learning.

Claude Bernard

It's what you learn after you know it all that counts.

Harry Truman

A man, though wise,
   should never be ashamed
   of learning more.
                                    Sophocles

I learn from anyone, but I
   do not stop at that. I go on
   trying to learn from myself.
                                    Zane Grey

I am still learning.
                        Michelangelo's Motto

Education is not a
preparation for life;
education is
life itself.

JOHN DEWEY

The years have much to teach which the days never know.

Ralph Waldo Emerson

There are some things you learn best in calm, and some in storm.

Willa Cather

A man should never stop learning, even on his last day.

Maimonides

Only the
educated
are free.

Epictetus

The excitement of learning
separates youth from old age.
As long as you're learning
you're not old.

Rosalyn Sussman Yalow

Never stop learning.
It keeps you young.

Patty Berg

The man who is too old
to learn was probably always
too old to learn.

Henry S. Haskins

The only sure weapon against bad ideas is better ideas. The source of better ideas is wisdom. The surest path to wisdom is a liberal education.

Alfred Whitney Griswold

The primary purpose of a liberal education is to make one's mind a pleasant place in which to spend one's leisure.

Sydney J. Harris

Education is the transmission of civilization.

ARIEL DURANT

He who opens
a school door
closes a prison.

Victor Hugo

Anyone who stops learning is old, whether at twenty or eighty.

HENRY FORD

In times of drastic change, it is the learners who inherit the future.

Eric Hoffer

LESSON #2

The Value of Hard Work

For all but the most gifted students, success in the classroom requires hard work. This is good. The ability to overcome procrastination and laziness is a skill that is best learned early in life. School provides a wonderful opportunity to convey the lesson that hard work pays great dividends.

Benjamin Franklin observed, "Diligence makes good luck." The best teachers convey Franklin's message, and thus prepare their students for a world that rewards effort just as surely as it punishes sloth.

If the power to do hard work is not talent, it is the best possible substitute for it.

JAMES A. GARFIELD

It is the first of all problems
for a man to find out what
kind of work he is to do
in this universe.

Thomas Carlyle

The one predominant duty
is to find one's work and do it.

Charlotte Perkins Gilman

No man is born whose work
is not born with him. There is
always work, and tools to work
with, for those who will.

James Russell Lowell

Talent is cheaper than
table salt. What separates the
talented individual from the
successful one is a lot
of hard work.

Stephen King

My success just evolved
from working hard at the
business at hand each day.

Johnny Carson

Every man's work is always
a portrait of himself.

Samuel Butler

Experience shows that
success is due less to ability
than to zeal. The winner is he
who gives himself to his
work, body and soul.

Charles Buxton

Creativity is a fancy word
for the work I have to do
between now and Tuesday.

Ray Kroc

I've always believed that
if you put in the work,
the results will come.

Michael Jordan

There is no great achievement
that is not the result of patient
working and waiting.

J. G. Holland

There is no obstacle in the
path of young people who are
poor, or members of minority
groups, that hard work and
preparation cannot cure.

Barbara Jordan

Success depends in a very
large measure upon individual
initiative and cannot be
achieved except by hard work.

Anna Pavlova

No person who
is enthusiastic
about his work
has anything to
fear from life.

SAMUEL GOLDWYN

God has a plan for all of us,
but He expects us to do our
share of the work.

Minnie Pearl

God gives every bird its food,
but he does not throw it
into the nest.

J. G. Holland

I like work; it fascinates me.
I can sit and look at it
for hours.

Jerome K. Jerome

There will always be a frontier where there is an open mind and a willing hand.

CHARLES F. KETTERING

He that is good for making
excuses is seldom good
for anything else.

Benjamin Franklin

Words without actions are
the assassins of idealism.

Herbert Hoover

There is no moment like the
present. The person who will
not execute his resolutions
when they are fresh upon
him can have no hope
from them afterwards.

Marie Edgeworth

Nothing is so fatiguing
as the eternal hanging-on of
an uncompleted task.
William James

This is a world of action and
not one of moping
or idleness.
Charles Dickens

Work is often the
father of pleasure.
Voltaire

When work is a pleasure,
life is a joy! When work
is a duty, life is slavery.

Maxim Gorky

Laziness may appear
attractive, but work
gives satisfaction.

Anne Frank

A life of ease is
a difficult pursuit.

William Cowper

All work and
no play makes
Jack a dull boy.
All play and no
work makes Jack
a mere toy.

MARIA EDGEWORTH

To love what you do
  and feel that it matters...
  how could anything
  be more fun?
Katharine Graham

Inspiration comes from
  working every day.
Charles Baudelaire

Trust your instincts.
  And never hope more
  than you work.
Rita Mae Brown

LESSON #3

The Importance of Character

A wise person once observed that if honesty did not exist, mankind would be forced to invent it in order to conduct human affairs.

Such is the importance of integrity that it comprises the very foundation of social interaction.

Teachers teach character by word and by example. These priceless lessons in integrity, once thoroughly learned, change the learner.

Forever.

Keep true, never be ashamed
    of doing right; decide on
    what you think is right
        and stick to it.

George Eliot

Never mind your happiness.
        Do your duty.

Will Durant

If a man seeks greatness,
    let him forget greatness
    and ask for truth, and
        he will find both.

Horace Mann

Fame is vapor,
popularity an
accident, riches take
wings. Only one
thing endures, and
that is character.

HORACE GREELEY

Truth will rise above
falsehood as oil
above water.

Cervantes

A quiet conscience
makes one so serene.

Lord Byron

Of all the properties which
belong to honorable men, not
one is so highly prized
as that of character.

Henry Clay

Reason often makes mistakes, but conscience never does.

JOSH BILLINGS

We do not need more
knowledge, we need
more character!
Calvin Coolidge

Character, not circumstances,
makes the man.
Booker T. Washington

Character builds slowly,
but it can be torn down
with incredible swiftness.
Faith Baldwin

Simplicity of character
is the natural result
of profound thought.
William Hazlitt

A man without ethics
is a wild beast loosed
upon this world.
Manly Hall

A man of character finds
a special attractiveness in
difficulty, since it is only
by coming to grips with
difficulty that he can
realize his potentialities.
Charles DeGaulle

Character consists
of what you do on
the third and
fourth tries.

JAMES MICHENER

Character isn't inherited.
One builds it daily by the
way one thinks and acts,
thought by thought,
action by action.
Helen Gahagan Douglas

Wherever a man goes,
his character goes with him.
African Proverb

Two things profoundly impress
me: the starry heavens above
me and the moral law
within me.
Immanuel Kant

Today, I am going to give you two tests: one on trigonometry and one on honesty. I hope you pass them both, but if you must fail one, let it be trigonometry.

MADISON SARRATT

LESSON #4

Kindness

Mother Teresa once observed, "Kind words can be short and easy to speak, but their echoes are truly endless."

And so it is that the teacher who makes kindness an integral part of the lesson plan leaves the world forever changed.

Teachers and non-teachers alike do well when they sow seeds of kindness. Those seeds, once sown, regenerate themselves in countless ways and touch the collective soul of mankind.

Those who learn
to love deeply never
grow old; they may
die of old age, but
they die young.

ARTHUR WING PINERO

None is so
near the gods as
when he shows
kindness.

SENECA

He who sows courtesy reaps
friendship, and he who plants
kindness reaps love.

Richard Brooks

The only gift is
a portion of thyself.

Ralph Waldo Emerson

When you're not thinking
about yourself, you're
usually happy.

Al Pacino

Kind words do not cost
much. Although they cost
little, they accomplish much.
Kind words produce
a beautiful image
on men's souls.

Pascal

You can't hold a man
down without staying
down with him.

Booker T. Washington

Help thy brother's boat
across, and lo! thine own
has reached the shore.

Hindu Proverb

Sympathy is never wasted
except when you give it
to yourself.

John W. Raper

Any fool can criticize,
condemn, and complain —
and most fools do.

Dale Carnegie

I feel an earnest and humble
desire, and shall do till I die,
to increase the stock of
harmless cheerfulness.

Charles Dickens

The best portion of a
   good man's life: his little,
nameless, unremarkable acts
   of kindness and love.

William Wordsworth

No act of kindness,
   no matter how small,
      is ever wasted.

Aesop

Never lose a chance
   of saying a kind word.

William Makepeace Thackeray

All who would win joy must share it; happiness was born a twin.

Lord Byron

LESSON #5

Self-worth

Comedienne Lucille Ball was once asked to share the best advice she had learned over a long and eventful life. Lucy responded simply, "Love yourself first." Teachers everywhere understand that message.

All too often, students enter the classroom with lowered self-esteem; in such cases, thoughtful teachers seek to infuse those students with a heightened sense of self-worth. Lessons in self-esteem are seldom found in textbooks, but such lessons are, in some cases, more important than the assigned schoolwork.

Teachers understand that all their students have value (even when the students themselves believe otherwise). The following quotations provide a brief refresher course for recognizing self-worth.

Those whom you can make
like themselves better
will, I promise you,
like you very well.
Lord Chesterfield

Too many people overvalue
what they're not and
undervalue what they are.
Malcolm Forbes

I think somehow we learn
who we really are and live
with that decision.
Eleanor Roosevelt

He who respects himself is safe from others; he wears a coat that none can pierce.

HENRY WADSWORTH LONGFELLOW

One face to the world,
  another at home,
  makes for misery.

Amy Vanderbilt

Nobody can make
  you feel inferior without
  your consent.

Eleanor Roosevelt

For an impenetrable shield,
  stand inside yourself.

Henry David Thoreau

When one is estranged from
oneself, then one is estranged
from others, too.
Anne Morrow Lindbergh

Choose a self
and stand by it.
William James

If you can't imitate him,
don't copy him.
Yogi Berra

No one can figure out
  your worth but you.
            Pearl Bailey

If you're going to take
  gambles, you must have one
    thing: self-confidence.
              Don Shula

Laugh at yourself,
  but don't doubt yourself.
    Be bold.
              Alan Alda

You must discover
who you are, and you must
trust your discovery.
Barbara Streisand

The promises of this world
are, for the most part,
vain phantoms; and to
confide in one's self and
become something of
worth and value is the
best and safest course.
Michelangelo

Make the most
of yourself, for
that is all there
is of you.

RALPH WALDO EMERSON

LESSON #6

Disciplined Behavior

Every teacher must, from time to time, face the challenge of classroom discipline.

Students, after all, are only human, and they sometimes express their humanity through unruly behavior.

It takes a mature teacher to convey the value and the power of self-discipline. The wisdom of disciplined behavior is a lesson that some students never learn, but those who do learn it are transformed.

Perhaps the most valuable
result of all education is the
ability to make yourself do the
thing you have to do when it
has to be done, whether
you like it or not.

Aldous Huxley

Education is teaching
children to behave as they
prefer not to behave.

Anonymous

The great business of man
is to improve his mind and
govern his manners.

Pliny

The important thing
  is to know how to take
    all things quietly.
                    Michael Faraday

The test of good manners
  is the ability to put up
    with bad ones.
                    Wendell Willkie

Self-control is the
  highest form of rulership.
                    Apocrypha

Obedience is
the gateway through
which knowledge,
yes, and love, too,
enter the mind
of a child.

ANNE SULLIVAN

Self-control is
 the hardest victory.

Aristotle

Whenever you are angry,
be assured not only that your
 anger is a present evil, but
 also that you have
 increased a habit.

Epictetus

Keep cool; anger is
 not an argument.

Daniel Webster

Discipline of the school
should proceed from
the life of the school as
a whole and not directly
from the teacher.

John Dewey

By constant self-discipline
and self-control you can
develop greatness of character.

Grenville Kleiser

Success isn't measured
by money or power
or social rank. Success
is measured by your
discipline and inner peace.

Mike Ditka

Some people
regard discipline
as a chore.
For me, it is
a kind of order
that sets me
free to fly.

JULIE ANDREWS

Good discipline
is a series of little
victories in which a
teacher, through
small decencies,
reaches a child's
heart.

HAIM GINOTT

LESSON #7

The Ability to Think

Students need their daily dose of reading, writing, and arithmetic, but a thorough education requires more than memorization. A student is not truly educated until he or she acquires the ability to think.

Alvin Toffler writes, "The illiterate of the future will not be the person who cannot read. It will be the person who does not know how to learn."

In a rapidly changing world, the invaluable teachers are those who teach their students how to think clearly and how to acquire new knowledge.

The great end of education
is to discipline rather than to
furnish the mind; to train it to
its own powers, rather than fill
it with the thoughts of others.

Tryon Edwards

Education is the methodical
creation of the habit of thinking.

Ernest Dimnet

Every man who rises above
the common level has received
two educations: the first from
his teachers; the second,
from himself.

Edward Gibbon

An education isn't how much you've committed to memory. It's being able to differentiate between what you do know and what you don't know.

William Feather

Education is knowing where to go to find out what you need to know; and it's knowing how to use the information you get.

William Feather

One of the strongest characteristics of genius is the power of lighting its own fire.

John Foster

If I have done the public
  any service, it is due
  to patient thought.

Sir Isaac Newton

The pursuit of the truth
  shall set you free —
  even if you never
  catch up with it.

Clarence Darrow

Time ripens all things;
  no man is born wise.

Cervantes

To learn is a natural pleasure
not confined to philosophers
but common to all men.

Aristotle

It is amazing what ordinary
people can do if they set out
without preconceived notions.

Charles F. Kettering

As long as you live,
keep learning how to live.

Seneca

Learning
without thought is
labor lost; thought
without learning
is perilous.

CONFUCIUS

A weak mind is like a microscope which magnifies trifling things but cannot receive great ones.

LORD CHESTERFIELD

Wisdom, thoroughly learned,
will never be forgotten.

Pythagoras

The easiest thing of all
is to deceive one's self:
for what a man wishes
he generally believes
to be true.

Demosthenes

Wise men learn more
from fools than fools
learn from the wise.

Cato

True wisdom lies in gathering
the precious things out of
each day as it goes by.

E. S. Bouton

Second thoughts
are ever wiser.

Euripides

If there is dissatisfaction
with the status quo, good.
If there is restlessness, I am
pleased. Then, let there be
ideas, and hard thought,
and hard work.

Hubert H. Humphrey

Read every day something
no one else is reading.
Think every day something
no one else is thinking.
It is bad for the mind to be
always part of unanimity.

Christopher Morely

Wisdom is the power that
enables us to use knowledge
for the benefit of ourselves
and others.

Thomas J. Watson

Experience is not what happens
to a man. It's what a man does
with what happens to him.

Aldous Huxley

Education should convert the mind into a living fountain and not a reservoir.

JOHN M. MASON

You can get help
from teachers, but
you are going to have
to learn a lot by
yourself, sitting
alone in a room.

DR. SEUSS

LESSON #8

Serving Others

The Golden Rule is alive and well: Man is at his best when he treats his fellows with the same care, dignity, and respect that he himself desires.

The quotations on the following pages point out the importance of service to others. Teachers, of course, have already learned this lesson (their chosen profession proves as much). Now what remains is for students to understand the value of generosity, cooperation, and sharing. These concepts, thoroughly learned, change not only the students but also the world.

Real education
should educate
us out of self into
something far finer:
into a selflessness
which links us
with all humanity.

NANCY ASTOR

A life isn't significant except for its impact on other lives.

JACKIE ROBINSON

Faith is the first factor in a
life devoted to service. Without
it, nothing is possible. With it,
nothing is impossible.

Mary McLeod Bethune

My dad has always
taught me these words:
care and share.

Tiger Woods

Nobody has one chance
in a billion of being thought
of as great after a century
has passed except those who
have been servants of all.

Harry Emerson Fosdick

We cannot live
only for ourselves.
A thousand fibers
connect us with
our fellow men.

HERMAN MELVILLE

Wisdom is often nearer
when we stoop than
when we soar.
William Wordsworth

There is nothing to make you
like other human beings so
much as doing things
for them.
Zora Neale Hurston

Everybody wants to do
something to help, but
nobody wants to be first.
Pearl Bailey

Make a habit of two things:
to help; or at least
to do no harm.

Hippocrates

The purpose of human
life is to serve, to
show compassion, and
to help others.

Albert Schweitzer

The best minute you spend is
the one you invest in people.

Ken Blanchard

Make yourself necessary to somebody.

ARNOLD GLASGOW

Make your life a mission, not an intermission.

RALPH WALDO EMERSON

A man wrapped up in himself
makes a very small package.
Benjamin Franklin

When the heart is right,
the feet are swift.
Thomas Jefferson

No one is useless in this world
who lightens the burden of it
for someone else.
Charles Dickens

LESSON #9

The Art of Living

The ultimate goal of education is, of course, preparation for life. Thus, the greatest teachers are those who teach, by example, the art of living.

What follows is a collection of life-lessons that should be an integral part of every curriculum.

Students — and teachers — please take note.

The art of living is like all arts; it must be learned and practiced with incessant care.

GOETHE

A person has to
live with himself, and
he should see to it
that he always has
good company.

CHARLES EVANS HUGHES

Fear not that thy life shall
come to an end, but rather
fear that it shall never have
a beginning.

Cardinal Newman

I am not afraid of tomorrow,
for I have seen yesterday
and I love today.

William Allen White

The faster you go, the more
chance there is of stubbing
your toe, but the better
your chances of getting
somewhere.

Charles F. Kettering

The worst sorrows
in life are not in
its losses and
misfortune,
but its fears.

A. C. BENSON

Good temper, like a sunny
day, sheds a ray of brightness
over everything; it is the
sweetener of toil and the
soother of disquietude!

Washington Irving

Good humor is one of the
best articles of dress one
can wear in society.

William Makepeace Thackeray

Do not let yourself be
tainted with barren
skepticism.

Louis Pasteur

Worry is evidence
of an ill-controlled
brain; it is merely
a stupid waste of
time spent in
unpleasantness.

ARNOLD BENNETT

Be not afraid of life. Believe that life is worth living, and your belief will help create the fact.

WILLIAM JAMES

The work of art must seize upon you, wrap you up in itself and carry you away. It is the means by which the artist conveys his passion.

AUGUSTE RENOIR

We have no more right
  to consume happiness
  without producing it
than to consume wealth
  without producing it.
George Bernard Shaw

Think of the ills from
  which you are exempt.
Joubert

Waste no tears over
  the griefs of yesterday.
Euripides

You will become as small as
your controlling desire;
as great as your
dominant aspiration.

James Allen

Life never becomes
a habit to me.
It's always a marvel.

Katherine Mansfield

If you love life,
life will love you back.

Artur Rubinstein

The best way to prepare
for life is to begin to live.
Elbert Hubbard

Write on your heart that
every day is the best day
of the year.
Ralph Waldo Emerson

The longer I live,
the more beautiful
life becomes.
Frank Lloyd Wright

Life is either a daring adventure or nothing.

HELEN KELLER

Endeavor to live so that
when you die, even the
undertaker will be sorry.

Mark Twain

When life kicks you,
let it kick you forward.

E. Stanley Jones

Life is 10 percent what
you make it and 90 percent
how you take it.

Irving Berlin

Life is what
we make it.
Always has been.
Always will be.

GRANDMA MOSES

The greatest use
of a life is to
spend it for
something that
will outlast it.

WILLIAM JAMES

Time is a circus always
    packing up and
    moving away.

Ben Hecht

One today is worth
    two tomorrows.

Benjamin Franklin

When you're green you're
growing; when you're
    ripe you rot.

Ray Kroc

Think of what you can do
with what there is.

Ernest Hemingway

In the long run, we hit
only what we aim at.
Aim high.

Henry David Thoreau

What we are is God's gift
to us. What we become is
our gift to God.

Eleanor Powell

This time, like
all times, is a very
good one if we
only know what
to do with it.

RALPH WALDO EMERSON

We are born weak, we need
strength; helpless, we need
aid; foolish, we need reason.
All that we lack at birth, all
that we need when we come
to man's estate, is the gift
of education.

Jean Jacques Rousseau

Hopefully, your education
left much to be desired.

Alan Gregg

No matter how long
you live, die young.

Elbert Hubbard

Sources

Sources

About the Author

Criswell Freeman is a Doctor of Clinical Psychology living in Nashville, Tennessee. He is the author of *When Life Throws You a Curveball, Hit It* and *The Wisdom Series* from WALNUT GROVE PRESS. He is also the author of numerous quotation books published by DELANEY STREET PRESS.

About
DELANEY STREET PRESS

DELANEY STREET PRESS publishes books designed to inspire and entertain readers of all ages. DELANEY STREET books are distributed by Walnut Grove Press. For more information, call 1-800-256-8584.